Paul Laurence Dunbar

Paul Laurence Dunbar

Poet Laureate of the Negro Race

Alice Dunbar Nelson,
William S. Scarborough and
Reverdy C. Ransom

MINT EDITIONS

Paul Laurence Dunbar: Poet Laureate of the Negro Race was first published in 1914.

This edition published by Mint Editions 2021.

ISBN 9781513224930 | E-ISBN 9781513223339

Published by Mint Editions®

MINT EDITIONS

MintEditionBooks.com

Publishing Director: Jennifer Newens
Design & Production: Rachel Lopez Metzger
Project Manager: Micaela Clark
Typesetting: Westchester Publishing Services

Contents

The Poet and His Song

Alice Dunbar Nelson

"Our notions upon the subject of Biography," says Carlyle, "may perhaps appear extravagant; but if an individual is really of consequence enough to have his life and character for public remembrance, we have always been of opinion that the public ought to be made acquainted with all the inward springs and relations of his character. How did the world and the man's life, from his particular position, represent themselves to his mind? How did coexisting circumstances modify him from without; how did he modify these from within? With what endeavors and what efficacy rule over them; with what resistance and what suffering sink under them? . . . Few individuals, indeed, can deserve such a study; and many *lives* will be written, and, for the gratification of innocent curiosity, ought to be written, and read and forgotten, which are not, in this sense, *biographies*."

Thus Carlyle. It would seem then, that if one must write about a poet, the world would wish to know how and in what manner the great phenomena of Nature impressed him, for Nature is the mother of all poets and there can be no true poetry unless inspired deeply by the external world which men do not touch. If the poet was an urban child, if the wonder of star-filled nights, the mystery of the sea, the beauty of sunrise and sunset, the freshness of dewy morns, and the warm scent of the upturned sod filled him with no rapture, then he was no true poet, howsoever he rhymed. So if one wishes to get a correct idea of any poet whatever, he must delve beneath the mere sordid facts of life and its happenings; of so many volumes published in such and such a time; of the influence upon him of this or that author or school of poetry; of the friends who took up his time, or gave him inspiration, and, above all, one must see what the love of Nature has done for the poet.

Mere looking into the printed words may not always do this. Who knows what heart-full of suggestion may lie in one expression? Who can tell in how much one word may be, as Higginson has expressed it, "palaces to dwell in," "years of crowded passion in a phrase," "half a life concentrated in a sentence?" To the banal mind a phrase may be nothing but a sweet rhythm of language, a well-turned, well-chosen expression. To the one who may have had the chance of communion with the creative mind, ere it expressed its longings in words, the phrase may be all pregnant with suggestion.

Your true poet is a child of Nature and lies close to the great Mother-heart. Even though he were born in the city, where his outlook on trees and fields is an incidental and sporadic occurrence in his life, he senses the divine heart pulsing beneath all things, and when he is finally brought face to face with the wonders of out-of-doors, untouched by the desecrating hand of man, he bursts forth into song, released from the conventionalities of other men's verse.

This was true of Paul Dunbar. He was a child of the city, a small city, true, where Nature was not so ruthlessly crushed away from the lives of men. There were trees and flowers near home, and a never-to-be-forgotten mill-race, which swirled through all his dreams of boyhood and manhood. Like the true poet that he was, he reached out and groped for the bigness of out-of-doors, divining all that he was afterwards to see, and in his earlier verse expressing his intuitions, rather than his observations.

Love of nature was there, but the power to express this love was not. Instead, he harked back to the feeling of the race, and intuitively put their aspirations into song. Tennyson and Lowell meant much to him, because they had expressed his yearnings for the natural world, and his soul yearned toward their verse. The exquisite line, "When cows come home along the bars—" how much of the English poet went into that line, and how much of the reminiscences of the earlier life of his family? More of the former, he always confessed.

Children love "The Seedling." It is good for them who are being initiated, city-wise, into the mysteries of planting and growth. It is scientific, without being technical—it is Tennyson's "Flower in the crannied wall," Americanized, brought down to the minds of little folks. The poet loved Tennyson, he walked with him in his earlier years, he confessed his indebtedness to him in his later days; he always praised him, and defended him hotly against the accusation of too much mere academic phrasing.

In the poem "Preparation" we see more of this groping toward the light; the urban child trying to throw off the meretriciousness of city life. Say what you will, or what Mr. Howells wills, about the "feeling the Negro life esthetically, and expressing it lyrically," it was in the pure English poems that the poet expressed *himself*. He may have expressed his race in the dialect poems; they were to him the side issues of his work, the overflowing of a life apart from his dearest dreams. His deepest sorrow he told in "The Poet."

He sang of life serenely sweet,
With now and then a deeper note.
From some high peak, nigh, yet remote,
He voiced the world's absorbing heat.

He sang of love when earth was young,
And love itself, was in its lays,
But, ah, the world, it turned to praise
A jingle in a broken tongues.

This is a digression. "Preparation" is contemporaneous with "Discovered" and "Delinquent," but in "the latter poems, he is feeling his way to make the laughter that the world will like; in the former, he is feeling his way to that true upward expression of the best in him. "A little bird sits in the nest and sings" is too much of Lowell to be true, "But the note is a prelude to better things," reflecting as in solution the thought of the "Vision of Sir Làkunfal." Our poet cast the poem aside as a thing of no worth, nor is it, except as it glimpses a bit of the soul within, like Lowell's clod "reaching up to a soul in grass and flowers."

Then came the experience on the lake. It was a never-to-be-forgotten summer. Opportunity and youth combined with poetry and the unsuspected beauty of the inland sea. Nature burst upon him with a surge. He knew now to the full the beauty of the gray days that he had dimly sung; the wind rising along the lake reeds and shivering premonition into them; the moon scudding before the wind clouds like a pale wraith with flung-back hair; the storm, never so swift in its wrath as on the shores of a lake; these things entered into his soul like a revelation. This, then, was what it all meant—these quivering fears and wonders of the early spring. From a little boy, he confessed, the spring filled him with longings, unexpressed, vague, terrible, like the fears, of the night, which persisted long after manhood. What did it mean, this terrible loneliness, this longing for companionship, and disgust with mere human company? He knew now. Nature had called him, and he had not been able to heed her call, until the Lake told him how.

He had sung about "Merry Autumn" in the conventional manner; he had enumerated pictures in the "Song of Summah," and he had written many conventional spring poems, dialect and otherwise, from the point of view of the spectator, but now began that passionate oneness with Nature, that was not to leave him until he deliberately turned his back upon her.

Beginning with that summer, he began to learn how to store up pictures in the mind as Wordsworth did. He began, mind you, only began to vlearn how to accumulate experiences that would later burst red-hot in one phrase, one line, one stanza that combined a month's experiences, a season's joy, a year's longing in them. It is only the true poet-heart that can do this. Whether or not it may be able to express it in rhythm, or metre, or music, or painting, or express it at all, is a mere matter of no moment. If these accumulated experiences be stifled in the sweet darkness of the heart, that is no matter, they have been; it is enough.

This faculty of stored experiences swiftly phrased may be exquisitely traced in many a poem. There was in Washington a bare, red-clay hill, open to the sun, barren of shade on its highest point, steep of ascent, boldly near the sky—truly, almost a "heaven-kissing hill." Daily walks on the hill fulminate in one line in "Love's Apotheosis," the sun-kissed hill." The white arc light of the corner lamp, filtering through the arches of the maples on Spruce street, make for the tender suggestion in "Lover's Lane," where the lovers walk side by side under the "shadder-mekin'" trees. Up in the mountains of the Catskills, where the rain fell often in July days, more often than the lover of out-door sports would relish, there was one little phoebe-bird, who would sing plaintively through all the rain, ending with a mournful chirp when the sun shone out at last. His little song through the disappointing storm was infinitely cheering, and often finds expression in the song of the human bird who listened to him.

> *An' it's moughty ha'd a-hopin'*
> *W'en de clouds is big an' black,*
> *An' all de t'ings you's waited fu'*
> *Has failed—er gone to wrack—*
> *But des keep on a joggin' wid a little bit of song,*
> *De mo'n is alius brightah w'en de night's been long.*

"Keep a Song Up on De Way" enshrines both the little bird and the beloved water-fall that boomed all night under the windows. The first and third stanzas were merrily conceived and merrily written, a "compliment to the persistent bird."

Oh, de clouds is mighty heavy—

(The cloud wraiths used to creep down the mountain side and literally, camp in the front yard, so that one went stumbling about in the mixture of cloud and mist),

An' de rain is mighty thick;
Keep a song up on de way.
And de waters is a rumblin'
On de boulders in de crick,
Keep a song up on de way.
Fu' a bird ercross de road
Is a-singin' lak he knowed
Dat we people didn't daih
Fu' to try de rainy aih
Wid a song up on de way.

The power of keen observation grows in arithmetical ratio as the soul divests itself of the littlenesses of life, the mere man-made ambitions, the ignoble strivings after place. The poet found new joy in the patch-work greenery of the mountains spread out at his feet; in the lights and shades on the fields of rye and corn and wheat and buckwheat, making the mountains seem as if Mother Nature had cunningly embroidered a huge cover for her summer dress. When he discovered, on the first visit, that the ground of the potato fields was violet, he cried aloud for joy. It had been a hard struggle to see that the light turned violet in the shadows under the vines, but when the realization came home, it was an exquisite sensation, worthy to be enshrined in a tender line. Thereafter, the mountains meant more than they had before, and subsequent visits always held out a promise of new things to be keenly detected and shoutingly announced. The waterfall that droned all night, save when, swollen with pride by the rain, it roared; the rain pouring down slantwise through the skies across the fields; the clouds casting great shadows athwart the mountain sides may have been forgotten those summers, yet, trick-like, they return here and there in unexpected places, showing how deeply they had become a part of "that inward eye, which is the bliss of solitude," of which Wordsworth sings. "The bird's call and the water's drone," and the "water-fall that sang all night," from "The Lost Dream," were but single instances of the stored-up memories expressed years after the summers in the Catskills were themselves fragments of forgotten days.

In the little poem "Rain-Songs" he sings:

> *The rain streams down like harp-strings from the sky,*
> *The wind, that world-old harpist, sitteth by;*
> *And ever, as he sings his low refrain,*
> *He plays upon the harp-strings of the rain.*

This came long after the simile of the harp-strings had been discovered, exulted over and laid aside on the tables of his memory. One more recollection of those days in the mountains is worth recording. The first time the song of the whip-poor-will came to him, he was amused. Plaintive it is to all who hear it for the first time, but to him it suggested tattling, from its nervous haste, its gasping intake of breath, like a little boy trying to clear himself from fault, yet half pleading that his companion in misdeeds be let go unpunished. The poet queried with much anxiety of everyone on the place, was the cry "Whip-poor-will" a command, or was it "Whip-poor-will" a pathetic question and hoping of Will's final exoneration? It was a whimsical turn that he gave to the cry of the night-bird, and the shrill insistence of the katy-did in the little poem "Whip-poor-Will and Katy-Did," when he wants to know why one must "Whip-poor-Will," when we know from the song of the insect that it was Katy who did?

This humorous outlook on Nature is a quaint turn of mind that few poets posses. Nature is stern, awful, sweet, sympathetic, lovable, but hardly humorous, so the world thinks. Yet where are there such exquisite manifestations of humor to be found in the man-made world about us? Nature's humor is grim sometimes, tricksy sometimes, dainty ofttimes, and sternly practical many times. To view life with humor is as Nature intended us to do. The gods must laugh, else where did men learn how?

This apropos of West Medford, Massachusetts. Here he visited thrice, and confessed that the place held for him the charm of hallowed association, which all the country near Boston must have for the world born outside Massachusetts, which still rules the minds of the *hoi polloi* with the potent sway of the nearest approach in this country to anything like reposeful ease and culture. But historic spots and monuments and powder mills of Revolutionary fame and battlefields meant but little after a while to the poet. Middlesex county abounds in rivers—were they fishable? Fishing was his one pastime, which he loved ardently, passionately, with the devotion of the true fisherman. Was there a river? Then the next question, "How is the fishing?" Walton's "Compleat Angler," is all right to read, but better to live. Anyhow it contains too many recipes for cooking. Van Dyke's "Fisherman's Luck" is better, particularly as the book is dedicated to the "Lady in Gray." Fishing and the color gray! His favorite sport and color; an unforgettable combination.

So the streams in the Catskills were deliciously suggestive of mountain trout, and even native indolence and poor health did not prevent him from arising one Fourth of July morning at three o'clock, and taking with him all the valiant souls who would go, to hie them to an over-fished stream, where the most carefully chosen flies only made the trout sniff and flirt themselves arrogantly; and where the unsportsmanlike women, having found a cool pool to use as a refrigerator, were stupid enough to try to tempt sophisticated suckers to bite—and that after a fierce cannonading of fire-crackers in honor of their early patriotism.

So West Medford suggested fishing, wonderful possibilities. What though Longfellow had enshrined the Mystic in the Hall of Fame by the lines in Paul Revere's Ride? That was no matter. Anything as brown and dimpled and slow as that river must be fishable. Thus he decided on his first visit and came back to investigate when there was more time, and lo! The result he humorously enshrined in the "Ballade."

> *By Mystic's bank I held my dream,*
> *(I held my fishing rod as well);*
> *The vision was of dace and bream,*
> *A fruitless vision, sooth to tell.*
>
> * * * * *
>
> *Oh, once loved, sluggish, darkling stream,*
> *For me no more thy waters swell,*
> *Thy music now the engines' scream,*
> *Thy fragrance now the factory's smell.*
>
> * * * * *
>
> *Thy wooded lanes with shade and gleam*
> *Where bloomed the fragrant asphodel.*
>
> * * * * *

Poor Mystic! "Arcadia now has trolley lines," mourns the poet, and so wends his way home to put up his fishing rod, and pack away the reel until the streams of the Rocky Mountains lure the basket and rod out again.

To the soul born inland, the sea is always a revelation, and a wonder-working experience in the life. The man born near the sea, who has been reared near its beauty and wonder, whose soul has learned early in life to enter into its moods, to understand its gentleness and not to fear its grimness, whose life has been attuned to the roar of the breakers and the purl of its littlest white waves, such a man can scarcely understand the rush and uplift that comes to the inland man who sees the ocean in his maturity for the first time. Such was the tidal wave that swept over the poet when the ocean burst upon his view. And like all those born inland, when once the fascination of the sea possesses them, it becomes more exquisitely a part of the whole nature than even it does in the case of the one born on the shores of the sea. When the sea became a part of the poet's life, it wrapped itself naturally into his verse—but hardly ever disassociated from the human element. Humanity and the ocean melted into one indistinguishable mist, even as Wordsworth's moors were always peopled with one shadowy figure so indistinct that it merged into the grayness of the horizon. There is no hint of the sea, save from the hearsay point, in the first published volume of poems, but before the second came, Narragansett Pier had opened his eyes to the mystic beauty of the ocean, and his soul to its turbulence. The journey to England made him familiar with the gray nothingness of mid-ocean, and life subsequently meant frequent pilgrimages to the seashore. Gray skies and gray sea; these meant most to him; sombreness and gloom seemed part of the real meaning of the ocean. One need not seek in the life of the poet a kinship between love of the serious aspects of nature and a fancied wrong or injury in life. Because Milton always loved the moon veiled in clouds is no reason why we should conclude that early and unfortunate loves left him unable to view skies moonlit and cloudless without sorrow. Because Keats found passionate intensity of emotion in the mere aspect of Grecian beauty, a passion that saddened him, is no reason why we should conclude that Greece had wronged him or that beauty had wrecked his life. A poet is a poet because he *understands*; because he is born with a divine kinship with all things, and he is a poet in direct ratio to his power of sympathy.

Something of this, emanating from his own experience the poet shows in his poem "Sympathy."

"I know what the caged bird feel, alas!"

The iron grating of the book stacks in the Library of Congress suggested to him the bars of the bird's cage. June and July days are hot. All out of doors called arid the trees of the shaded streets of Washington were tantalizingly suggestive of his beloved streams and fields. The torrid sun poured its rays down into the courtyard of the library and heated the iron grilling of the book stacks until they were like prison bars in more senses than one. The dry dust of the dry books (ironic incongruity!—a poet shut up in an iron cage with medical works), rasped sharply in his hot throat, and he understood how the bird felt when it beat its wings against its cage.

When he went down to Arundel-on-the-Bay—picturesque name of a picturesque place—he was thrilled as though stepping on hallowed ground. This was the Eastern Shore that gave birth to Douglass. More than the Boston Common, which memorized Attucks and deified Robert Gould Shaw and inspired his best sonnets, this was near the home of the idol of his youthful dreams, the true friend of his enthusiastic youth. The place was wild after the fashion of the shore of the Chesapeake; it seemed almost home to him—and the fishing was excellent. He enshrined it in his memory, and later came the poem "The Eastern Shore." It was written months after the lure of the bay had been forgotten when the skies swirled snow down on a shivering city, and the mind warmed the body as it harked back to the hot days of July under the burning skies and over the clean-washed sands of the Chesapeake Bay. One more poem the eastern shore inspired, "The Memory of Martha." The story "The Memory of Martha" being finished, the poet found himself rushed onward with a mighty sympathy for the man he had created, whose wife had left him for the unknown. It was the poet-heart throbbing in sympathy with the woes of the universe. He *was* the old husband, mourning his loss, even as when he wrote "Two Little Boots"; he *was*, for the time being, the broken-hearted mother, mourning over the little shoes. He wept as he wrote the poem, both poems in fact, and then laughed at his own tears—no immediate animus for either poem, just the overflowing of an understanding soul over a fancied grief.

Sometimes with him the memory of the words of another author commingled with a landscape, and then there is a rare combination of verse. It was when in the dire grip of pneumonia that the oft-reiterated desire, perhaps delirious, certainly comic, came for "A bear story, just one little bear story," to be read aloud to him. Blessed fortune it was then that Ernest Thompson-Seton was just giving to the world his inimitable "Wild Animals I Have Known," and fever or no fever, the poet must revel into forgetfulness of pain in listening to the woes of Raggy-lug, and the too canny wolves and bears. It made a review of the "Jungle Book" a delightful process, and invited a re-persual of Bliss Carman's poems. When the Catskills burst upon his delighted vision a while later, what more natural than that "To the Road," with its hint of Carman should enshrine the little white road winding up the mountain side?

> Cool is the wind, for the summer is waning—
> Who's for the road?
> Sun-flecked and soft where the dead leaves are raining,
> Knapsack and alpenstock press hand and shoulder—

Merriment here, loud and long, because any old dead branch when carried on a walk became dignified by the name of alpenstock, and the leather chatelaine purse of the companion in tramping became a knapsack.

The "Forest Greeting" enshrined both Kipling and Thompson-Seton. "Good Hunting," from the cry of the wood brothers in the "Jungle Book," but the mourning was for the wounded animals, the funeral wail of the little ones left alone to whose sufferings Thompson-Seton was the first to call attention in an unsentimental way.

All this newly-acquired love of the wee things of Nature and life had taught him to let the smallest suggestions find expression in the quaintest turns of comic verse. The east winds from the Massachusetts Bay howl around the houses of West Medford, and their piercing "Woo—oo—ee!" suggested the "Boogah Man," written for the very tiny maiden of two years, who persisted in hugging his avuncular shoes when he wanted to write sonnets about Harriet Beecher Stowe and Robert Gould Shaw. How can one work? he asked fretfully, and then burst laughingly into "How's a poet to write a sonnet, can you tell?" And so dashed off the poem on scrap paper, and read it aloud to the small maiden, who thereupon suggested that the "Woo—oo" of the wind was a "Boogah Man." So that was written immediately, dramatizing it as he wrote, much to her delight.

The dramatic instinct was strong behind the delicate perception of the power of suggestion. One must dramatize the poems as they were written, white hot. So, when "The Dance" and "The Valse" were penned, the metre must be dramatized in order to get it right; anapestic tetrameter admits of no limping lines; so one must waltz, humming the lines in order that there be no faulty rhythm. It was well that there were good dancers in the household to be sure there would be correct metre. "Whistling Sam" was troublesome. All had to whistle Sam's tunes, and then the music teacher must come and play them out on the piano, and transcribe the musical notation to be sure there were no mistakes.

Suggestion—that power of making one idea bring out a poem apparently foreign to the original thought—was never more humorously exemplified than in "Lias" and "Dat Ol' Mare o' Mine," both products of that winter in Colorado. "Dat Ol' Mare" was a weird and eccentric maiden horse of uncertain age and dubious ancestry, whose ideas were diametrically opposed to any preconceived notions one might suppose horses in general and Colorado horses in particular to have. But she would come home "on de ve'y da'kest night," without guidance, even if she did betray doubtful pre-ownership in the day-time when an exasperated and embarrassed woman drove her into Arapahoe street, the end of the ranch road, upon which street she would make frequent, unpsychological and embarrassing stops. But she would come home unguided and sure, hence "Dat Ol' Mare o' Mine."

There never was a "Lias," except generically, but maternal adjurations as to the beauty of the life of the despised early worm, and the "early to rise" maxim generally was greeted with Homeric laughter, and culminated in poor abused "Lias."

Colorado! As much of a revelation of Nature as the sea! But here was a new mother, more stern, less sure, never so capable of intimacy. Magnificent sweep of mountain range visible from the windows of the tiny house on the ranch—one hundred and fifty miles of Rocky Mountains, from Pil e's Peak to Long's Peak, with all the unnamed spurs in between! Unsurpassed sunsets, wonderful sunrises that flushed the eastern prairies, and reflected back on the snows of the mountains in the west so that the universe went suffused in a riotous prismatic color scheme; the meadow lark perched on the eaves of the house, tossing golden liquid sweetness to the high clear heavens; cowboys herding unwilling cattle across the horizon, miles and miles away; clear ozone, thin air which pierced the lungs and made them expand, sharp extremes in January from 60 degrees above to 30 degrees below. Here was Nature, untamed, unconfined, unfamiliar, wild. It went to the head like new wine, and ideas came rushing, fulminating, fructifying. One forgot sometimes, and it became comic when forgetting that the altitude of Denver and the surrounding land of 5200 feet or more was just becoming familiar; one rushed fearlessly into the higher strata of other towns, like Leadville and Colorado Springs, and was brought sharp up against the stubborn fact that rarity of air is not to be tampered with by the tenderfoot.

But the longing for the beloved East persisted, and though two novels and some short stories came forth that winter, the verse halted because the heart was elsewhere. "A Warm Day in Winter" and "Spring Fever" are both suggestive of the East, yet both were descriptive of days in Harmon. In the darkness of the night came the sound of a herd of cattle, padding feet echoing through closed doors, and so the simile of a race struggling slowly through the dark was born, and the poem "Slow Through the Dark" came to life:

> *Slow moves the pageant of a climbing race;*
> *Their footsteps drag far, far below the height—*

The spectacle of a small caravan climbing the heights of the mountains in the far distance, up the steep winding road that crept whitely out of sight across the snow-capped boulders, was pregnant with the same suggestion. So came to his mind "By Rugged Ways":

> *By rugged ways and through the night*
> *We struggle blindly toward the light.*

These two poems were always among his favorites. The darker side of the problems of the race life was being brought home more and more forcibly to him as he grew older, and the stern ruggedness of nature in the Rocky Mountains forced him to a realization of the grim problems of the world's work.

As the herd of cattle climbing the sides of the mountain suggested something more than insensate animals struggling toward food and shelter, so the trifle of a brick side yard, damp and shut in by high brick walls of the two houses on each side, made for a riot of odd little poems. There were many poems born out of the fulness of the heart, out of a suggestion of long ago, from a picture, from a book, from a chance expression. Many were truly lyrical in that they were the record of the "best and happiest moments," as Shelley puts it. So many were truly poetic in that they were the record of the divine oneness with all mankind and all nature, and so many were like that group of November poems in that they were merely experiments in the power of suggestion.

If a short brick walk between two brick walls of two city houses does not suggest a cloistered walk of a monastery, what, then, does it suggest? And if that walk be damp, as perforce it must be, and if violet beds grow on the side, wild rank things, pushing through the brick crevices and allowed to remain because the inmates of the house are sentimentally fond of violets—even wild ones that grow in city back yards—what more natural than that all kinds of cool, damp, cloistered ideas will emanate from the tiny spot? So in one *dies mirabilis* were born "To a Violet Found on All Saint's Day," "The Monk's Walk," "The Murdered Lover," "Love's Castle," "Weltschmertz," "My Lady of Castle Grand," and "In the Tents at Akbar."

It is a base libel, much advertised and bruited abroad, to label the exquisite "Violet Found on All Saints' Day" as a vulgar premonition, Within the one little flower was all the lesson of "The Seedling," fruition now, less Tennyson, more filled with the understanding of maturity. The poet had been told by those near him, who once had lived in a Roman Catholic community, that on All Saints' Day everyone goes to the cemeteries laden with flowers to lay on the graves of the loved lost ones. He had always loved the custom and he remembered each All Saints' Day with a tender sympathy. So he saw in the violet not a premonition of despair, but a sweet effort on its part to bloom in memory of man's sorrows.

The chill November winds, following an unusually riotously beautiful Indian summer, waved the bird's nest in the Virginia creeper on the house next door, and "Weltschmertz" came forth, his deepest sympathy with all the woe of the world—complete universality of the true poet, nothing personal, merely infinite. The line "Count me a priest" betrays its cloister sisterhood. "The Monk's Walk" was near enough to the original idea of a monastery, but it evolved into the "Murdered Lover." The little walk grew to mean cloisters, castles, priests, knights—even

"My Lady of Castle Grand," by the process of suggestion comes to life, for what so medieval as a castle with an inverted Lady of Shalott?

The medieval fancy ran riot then, and though it seems a far cry from Tennyson's "Lady of Shalott" to Bayard Taylor's "Bedouin Love Song," yet such a bridge does the poet's fancy make from reality to dreamland, that all strange fancies clustered about that cloistered walk, and his imagination careened out into the desert sands "In the Tents of Akbar," because the "Murdered Lover" of the poem, written in the morning, suggested the murdered dancing girl under the burning skies, and the grief of Akbar rent his heart in the evening. It is the exceptional mind that drags its pitifully methodical way through conventional, well-worn grooves of thought. One who thinks at all thinks by leaps and bounds, ranging all the universe, touching but tangentially the thought suggested by the last thought, and then winging swift flight elsewhere. Else wherefore think? One might as well ruminate. The poet puts wings to his words, as Homer phrases it, "winged words," and lo, a poem is born. And three or four great poems may have the same trivial place of conception, or a great soul-shaking experience may culminate in a line. Else why write poetry?

The power of Mother Nature having once entered into the poet-soul, it could never leave altogether. When the day came that he turned his back upon her deliberately, she did not avenge herself, but persisted in the haunting line, the pregnant phrase, the tender mood, albeit dimmer in each succeeding poem. For she gathers all her children to her breast and croons them melodies that will last through all eternity, if they will have them last; and even when the petulant children stop their ears, the inward ear listens to the great mother heart and heeds its call.

Wilmington, Del.

The Poet Laureate of the Negro Race

William S. Scarborough

William Dean Howells, Edmund Clarence, Stedman, Eugene Field, James Whitcomb Riley, James Lane Allen and Robert Ingersoll were the jury which named Paul Laurence Dunbar poet laureate of the Negro race.

Dr. Davis W. Clark, of Boston, in speaking of our poet, says: "But, when all is said, his true distinction lies in the fact that he interpreted the particular to the universal, the Negro to the whole human race. He demonstrated, too, by his own genius that the Negro also belongs to the divine family on earth, in spite of all prejudiced denial. He easily molded the white man's language into the modes of thought of the black man and *vice versa*; thus showing that they are interchangeable. So the community of genius is illustrated and proven. The accident of his seniority as the poet of his race would alone insure him a permanent place.

He is the first among ten million. Again, he did not inherit, he originated. His race had nothing to transmit in the way of literary or poetic instinct or training. That this young Negro should take up what has heretofore been the white man's own distinctive art, and excel and surpass in it, is the marvel of the hour. The Caucasian's wealth of literary inheritance and training of several millenniums seemed to give him no advantage over the meagerly furnished and heavily handicapped son of Ham. Right worthily, then, is Paul Laurence Dunbar 'laurel-decked.'"[1] Thus does Dr. Clark emphasize the appropriatness of the verdict of these eminent men.

The Unveiling of the Poet's Monument

It was June 26, 1909, that the white citizens of Dayton, Ohio, paid a tribute to the memory of the dead poet by unveiling a monument in his honor erected by popular subscription and locating it in harmony

---

1. An extract from the address delivered by Dr. D. W. Clark, of Boston, at the unveiling of the poet' monument in Dayton's most beautiful cemetery and on the most beautiful knoll in that cemetery. The other orator was the writer of this appreciation of the poet.

with the poet's expressed wish under a willow, near a pool of water and not beyond the noises of the road. (See "Death's Song.")

It was a beautiful sight, more than a thousand of Dayton's best citizens had gathered at his tomb that beautiful morning in June, seemingly vying with one another in paying respect to the memory of one of their most distinguished dead—Paul Laurence Dunbar. James Whitcomb Riley was there. It was he who whispered his condolence in the ear of the poet's mother over the long distance telephone, "not trusting his pen or waiting for the mail." Others eminent in poetry and prose and national in reputation were present to do honor to his memory. The Philharmonic Society—seventy in number—composed of Dayton's best white musicians, men and women, sang as hymns the poet's words set to music. It was indeed a gathering for an unusual purpose. It was not that a memorial to a great citizen was an extraordinary occurrence, for this is almost a daily happening. But it was a remarkable thing that such a gathering should be in memory of a man not only of humble birth, but one of the darker race—one with a sable skin, the badge of servitude and oppression that has been the Negro's lot for so many years. But on that day race and color were lost sight of and the Gem City of Ohio was proud to honor its distinguished son who had helped to give it fame—to honor him because of his worth, his genius, his work.

The old adage that a prophet is not without honor save in his own country is another instance of the falsity of so many popular sayings; for in that beautiful city where Paul Laurence Dunbar was reared, where he made his home and gathered to himself friends—here he was most highly honored; and in that memorial to him they not only did honor to an individual man of color who had lived and wrought so well as to deserve recognition by his fellows, but they did honor to an entire race, and to mankind regardless of race.

As I considered that splendid tribute to the Negro poet, as I dwelt upon the meaning of such an expression of appreciation of his greatness, my heart swelled with pride and gratitude that in this day and generation such a thing is possible. And I was more and more convinced that, after all, the possibilities of any race are to be finally determined by the heights reached by its men of intellect, of brain, of genius—men of power who are able to touch the hearts and stir the pulses of the world by their marvelous ability for delineation by pen, brush or chisel—men who rise in the realm of the fine arts and command the world to listen, to gaze, to admire, to respect, to praise their efforts. That tribute to

Dunbar by his white fellow citizens showed that after all genius is not a matter of race, color or condition, and that it will win its way forward and upward. The men and women who possess it are the ones who will raise a people to higher planes. These are the ones who will give this same people a place among the nations of the earth. These are the ones that we especially praise and honor.

But the Negro race has had such men scattered throughout its history—men of color who have distinguished themselves. We do not need to go back to the centuries when Bagay or Cugoano or Vassa lived for such material to declare the Negro's ability. The last century has given the world a *proud* list from which we may draw examples of Negro greatness in the higher walks of life.

I recall with pleasure the sight of a bronze figure in the *Place Malesherbes* of Paris which was the work of the great artist and sculptor Doré. It is that of Alexander Dumas *pere*, France's great Negro historical romancer, who has enchanted the world with his story-telling genius.

Dumas, the father, and Dumas, the son, both have carved a niche for the race where their names are imperishably written, and France is proud to honor them. Twenty-three years ago Russia did honor to another Negro as we did honor Dunbar five years ago. Then the statue of Alexander Pushkin, acknowledged as Russia's greatest poet, was unveiled in Moscow to an admiring people who celebrated thus the literary achievements of the Negro "poet of the Caucasus." Pushkin's name is immortal in Russian hearts.

Down the list we may come to touch Phyllis Wheatley, whose powers drew a tribute from George Washington; to Banneker, who astounded the world with his scientific astronomical calculations—down to the present where the names cluster more thickly, because of honors won; Edmonia Lewis, who from Rome made her fame as a sculptress and Henry Tanner, whose fame as an artist has reached the coveted recognition of the French Government. These, with Douglass and Washington and Du Bois, and a host of others, have proved to the world that the "Souls of Black Folk" differ not from other souls in high impulses, aspirations, and even genius.

Russia and France are proud of their sable writers, each of whom stamped his own personality upon the literature of his nation, and why should not America possess the same pride?

When we come down to modern times and review the field as it is stretched out before us, there is no literary character that stands higher than Paul Laurence Dunbar. We speak of Longfellow and Whittier and Bryant and Lowell, and other great American poets, and speak of them with rightful pride; but to my mind not one of them was a sweeter singer than Paul Laurence Dunbar. He sang with equal freedom and boldness, he sang with equal musical rhythm, he sang with their grace and beauty, and he sang of the desires, the struggles, the ambitions, the aspirations of a people that seemed to have no future. In his song he has helped pave the way for a future for his race. He has hewn out a path, has trodden the ground for others to follow, and what was possible in his case is possible for others.

The very fact that he made his way to the front from humble origin and against tremendous odds shows the *power of a soul*.

Paul Laurence Dunbar was no prodigy, no bundle of eccentricities, no Blind Tom whose powers in one direction were miraculous and balanced by the dwarfing of all else in his nature and character. He was a normal man in every respect and as such is to be judged as every other man of letters.

In all nations it is an accepted fact that the literature of a people is influenced by four things. The *race* of the writer is to be taken in consideration as well as the epoch in which he lives and the immediate *environment* about him. We do not except from this rule the one whose name we honored at the unveiling of the monument erected by popular subscription by his friends of the white race. Paul Laurence Dunbar was of African ancestry. It could not be claimed that a large percentage of his ability was due to the amount of Caucasian blood in his veins. He represented the Negro in America in letters as few others who have reached eminence could do. I would emphasize that his gift of song was pre-eminently racial. He had the happy gaiety and the weird imagination of his race. He sang from his heart as the race has sung ever since it was brought to these shores. It is shown in his dialect poems where the same wonderful combination of Aesopian wisdom and imaginative humor that have made Harris' African stories so famous is evidenced at every turn.

He felt for his race, and as his race he sang with the heart and tongue of his people. It was not all joy. Sorrow and sadness crept in. The changeful moods were his, and so his poems met the moods of mankind and won a place in hearts, which must be done to win a way to fame. He was a child of nature. The wind dared him to song: the spring warmed in his veins when the

> *"Grass commence a-comin'*
> *Throo de thawin' groun'."*

And summer lured him with the

> *"Pines a-smellin' in de wood."*

Like all other writers, he was also influenced by his *environment*, which here was closely allied to racial influence and had a strong sway over his works, imbuing them with the touch and personality that have made their peculiar charm.

Every phase of Negro life has been caught by his pen as by a camera. The simplest and homeliest life about him threw upon his brain indelible pictures that he transformed to liquid notes of song, sparkling with grace and vivid imagination. The life of the fireside, the field, the cabin, the wood, the stream—all gave him happy themes for his gift to play upon. The peculiar traits of his people, their quaint characteristics, their propensities and inclinations all received a loving, tender tribute at his hand as he wove them into immortal verse.

The third influence—the epoch—shows comparatively little influence over his works. Here and there we find him centralizing thought upon the spirit of the times about him. It was an age of peace in Dunbar's years, so his muse was not stirred to clarion tones, but when the blind rage of mob violence pursued his people, his "Talking Oak" showed how his heart was stirred; and when Frederick Douglass died he mourned in an elegy that showed the true poetic fire ablaze from the friction of life about him, but his prose has shown this influence of the world ideas about him far more than his poetry, for Dunbar's literary fertility was not confined to the poetic field alone.

Largely influenced by *race* and *environment* in his writings, yet one other influence that has always been the *mightiest* in the literature of any people was also his. This was *Genius*. We cannot account for genius in any people. It springs up and no one can trace it. It comes more often from the lowliest surroundings. The soul that comes from Nature's God, that lives close to Nature, that sees life clearly, that knows other souls by mysterious affinity—that soul is born and carries its possessor into the upper realms where but few can follow, and we call it *genius*.

Paul Laurence Dunbar had genius. Only a genius could have sung as he has sung, only a genius could have triumphed as he has triumphed, only a genius could have made a permanent place in American literature for himself as he has done. His death was untimely. His career was not completed. What might he not have done had more years been given him? But God—who took him—knew best. And here we may repeat that whatever definition we may give genius, the fact is that no man possessing such as Dunbar possessed can ever be kept down. Genius forces its way upward. It demands recognition. Dunbar's native powers forced the world to give him place and to sing his praises. I remember in Europe when, on a special occasion, his name was mentioned before an audience, that the people vied in enthusiastic applause for the black boy who had sung himself into prominence by the greatness of his intellectual powers. If this side of Negro life—the literary side—could be dwelt upon more, if the career made by one like Paul Laurence Dunbar could be held up more before the world, if the intellectual progress of the Negro could be taken up for consideration to a greater extent, and if the distance that he has come from the days of slavery to the present could form the subject of more speeches and orations, I feel very sure that the people of America would be willing to grant the black man a hearing and a more favorable consideration in the matters that make for the highest good of the race.

If the literature of Dunbar is taken upon its merits, we feel that both the prose and poetry of others of the race will be likewise favorably regarded, and in that sense the Negro people will be benefited. The lives of such men as Dunbar, Tanner and Du Bois, who have with others made a future for the people along higher lines, should inspire us all. There are many of the race here and there in nearly every city, building slowly but surely in literature and art and are making a way for those who are to follow.

Greatness does not come to every man even though he may work for it, but there are some who by their own power of mind and personality tower above the common people, thereby showing that greatness is limited to no one people and to no one class of people. Mr. Dunbar was one of this class. His life, as has been said, was a brilliant one in a literary sense. He was a prolific writer as well. The large number of volumes emanating from his pen and the great interest manifested by the public at large in his works clearly prove that his powers were fed from a perennial spring.

Their freshness and virility both astonished and pleased the waiting public, which continually called, like Oliver Twist, for more, and continually gave a spontaneous meed of praise for every new effort.

He died in the harness, so to speak, with a volume incomplete. Why the Creator saw fit to remove him from the scene of his earthly labors at his early age man cannot tell. We feel the loss as a race of a brilliant man and helper of his people. He has dropped his mantle. Upon whose shoulders it will fall, time alone can tell, but it is due his fame to say that we would eagerly applaud the singer of color who may prove worthy to wear it. We have lamented the loss of such men as Douglass and Crumwell and Payne, men on whom the years bore heavily, but Dunbar was young, in his prime, and greater things were to be achieved. We needed him, as we need all strong literary characters, to help a people to a standing place in the world of letters. Yet his life, his work—this memorial—all must ever be an inspiration to every Negro youth to set his feet in the paths for higher things, to be determined to win spurs in some great ambitious effort to compel the recognition of the world for some great achievement.

Every person of color should feel under lasting gratitude to our honored poet for the position he won for his people; and the race must never fail to show that gratitude, not only for this fact, but for every phase of recognition accorded him by other races.

I say his life, with its crown of laurel, should be an inspiration to the Negro people, and I also say that it should be a lesson for the critics of the race. To those who do well, the recognition befitting their merits should be given. As his mother had reason to be proud of such a son, so the City of Dayton had reason to be proud of such a citizen, and this great State of Ohio should feel itself also honored by such a career of such an illustrious citizen.

I considered it an honor that I was able on that occasion to, stand over his monument and in the name of the Negro people, and, in the name of humanity, thank all those of that great city who had joined to raise such a memorial to the honor of this sweet American bard, to thank them all regardless of race or color, who had risen to such heights in honoring this poet of sable hue, to congratulate all that race, color or creed was not allowed to dampen ardor or be an obstacle in honoring their fellow-townsman. Ohio was honored by that tribute. America was honored by it, and that day should ever be a proud one in the annals of that city and its people. There Dunbar spent his youth; there he developed his talent; there he laid down his work, and while we add a laurel leaf to the chaplet which fame placed upon his living brow, we declare that

> *"The great work laid upon his short years*
> *Is done, and well done."*

Such lives are blessings in the world at large. God lends them to the world to show that mind knows no race—that we are all brothers, differing from one another only as gifts and graces differ—that the Creator is our common Father through whose gracious kindness such lives spring up, blossom and bear fruit to prove the immortality of the soul.

Dunbar will never die, even though his body lies buried in the earth. His soul of song will continue to re-echo in the hearts of men, and the brightness and beauty, the humor and pathos, the tenderness and sympathy with which he has enriched the world will rest like a benediction upon us all for all time to come. Yes, Dunbar still lives in his songs and in our hearts—the same earnest, sincere, gentle, genial soul that we knew so well in his earthly years. His gentle spirit today hovers over the home he loved so well, and the city dear to his heart, and though he has gone to take his rest, that spirit will be a guardian angel, blessing all for the greatness of heart and soul that has evoked that tribute from a grateful, appreciative people.

His wish was fulfilled. He sleeps among his fellow-citizens, as he begged in his touching "Death Song."

> *"Let me settle w'en my shouldahs draps dey load*
> *High enough to hyeah de noises in de road;*
> *Fu' I t'ink de las' long res'*
> *Gwine to soothe my sperrit bes'*
> *Ef I's layin' 'mong de t'ings I's allus knowed."*

Personalia

BORN, DAYTON, OHIO, JUNE 27, 1872. Died, Dayton, Ohio, February 9, 1906. Mother, emancipated slave. Father, slave, escaped from Kentucky to Canada via underground railway. Educated Dayton common schools. Graduated, Steele High School, Dayton, 1891. Wrote class poem. Editor-in-chief *High School Times*, 1891. President Philomathean Society, 1891. Only colored man ever elected to above two positions. Clerk in Haytian Building, World's Fair, Chicago, 1893. Tendered a reception by the staff of the *Century Magazine*, New York,

Richard Watson Gilder presiding, 1896. Tour of England reading and reciting, 1896, eight months. Guest of the Hon. John Hay, Henry M. Stanley, the Savage Club, the Royal Geographical Society, etc., London 1897. Employments while in school, and early part of literary career, elevator boy, court page, and position in Congressional Library, Washington, D. C. Married Alice Moore, New York City, 1898. Miss Moore is a school teacher, short-story, magazine writer, and author of two volumes: "Violets and Other Tales," and "The Goodness of Saint Roque." His last dialect poem was entitled, "Sling Along." Among his last poems was one entitled, "Equipment." Four stanzas refer to himself. His last poem, one stanza, was addressed to his friend, Dr. Burns, who was also his physician and who died three months before Dunbar. These as yet unpublished.

Wilberforce University, Wilberforce, Ohio

Paul Laurence Dunbar

Reverdy C. Ransom

Paul Laurence Dunbar was a product of the first generation of freedom. Whatever of talent, endowment or genius he possessed belonged to the rich, warm blood of his African inheritance. We know that capacity, genius, ability, are not limited by race or blood; but so universal is the imputation of racial inferiority to the African and his descendants that the achievements of each gifted son or, daughter reflect glory upon the entire race. The Negro has contributed very little to what we know as human progress in the terms of modern civilization. This fact is used against him and is made to justify his unequal and degrading treatment. It is only by multiplying examples of the highest achievement that the universal judgment may be reversed. In the United States, Dunbar and Henry O. Tanner are "the sea mark of our farthest sail" in letters and in art. These are not freaks or prodigies, but prophecies of the latent powers of the race, the first unfoldings of which have not yet but fairly begun.

Like the midnight sun of the North Polar regions, the darkness that has enveloped the African and his descendants has been briefly illuminated here and there through the centuries by some bright Negro intellect in almost every quarter of the earth. However widely the many varieties of the human race may differ in certain physical characteristics, they have a common origin and are of one and the same family. The Creator has not made one branch of the human family inferior to another. History does, however, abundantly prove that the groups into which the human family is divided differ in race traits, characteristics and in wealth of endowment in certain specific directions. The world is indebted to the Jews for keeping alive and transmitting across the centuries a pure monotheism. The Greeks realized the highest ideal of beauty to which mankind has yet attained; while the white races of Europe and America have displayed a genius for colonization, commerce and invention applied to the development of the physical resources of the earth. So large and comprehensive have been the contributions to knowledge that it is felt by many that there is little left of a distinctive character for the black peoples to do. But in the spiritual realm, in the emotions, in music, in kindness, in cheerfulness and the spirit of brotherhood, the Negro has a wealth of endowment, which, when his hour comes, will put a living soul into the activities of human life which may well be the glory and the crown of that world-wide civilization which makes for peace, for brotherhood and love.

Dunbar was an interpreter of the life and spirit of his people. Fresh as a breath from the hills, his poems breathe with the atmosphere which surrounds the life of his race. Dunbar's voice is the first note of the bird that sounds the approach of dawn. He fell asleep before his eyes beheld the day which he had ushered in. But the harp whose strings were touched by him with such poetic grace will not remain forever silent. Other hearts that have been warmed by the equatorial sun will be filled with new and higher, inspirations; other hands, black tinseled by the subtle alchemy of the tropic's, will lift the veil from off the ability and power of his people, that all the world may feast its hollow metallic senses in the banqueting house of mind and spirit where the heart presides.

Dunbar was always a child—a child at play—who passed from us before he came to the full maturity of his powers. From the days of his boyhood, intimately and well we knew him, when he was yet unknown beyond a narrow circle in the busy little city where he held a position of the humblest sort. We have ridden with him many times in the car of his elevator, where, scattered about him on loose sheets of paper, were some of the first of his imperishable lines which were to win the admiration of the world. When his first book, "Oak and Ivy," came from the press, we introduced him to our congregation and assisted him in disposing of copies he had borrowed from the printer to pay the cost of publication. More than once have we dined with him, with chitterlings and hot corn pone as the piece de resistance. He has come to us in the late hours of the night, when the muses were singing at the windows of his soul, in search of a word that might better convey the delicate shades of thought or feeling they brought before his vision. The late John Bigelow said of a visit to Alexander Dumas, that Dumas showed him a story he had just completed, and in reply to a question, remarked that he never rewrote his manuscripts, but let the first draft stand. This, Bigelow gratuitously remarks, was "characteristic of his race." This was not true of Dunbar, who was three-fourths more Negro than Dumas. When the song had spent itself, he carefully corrected and revised. May we not add that this was "characteristic of his race"? Dunbar was the spoiled child of the agreeable men and winsome women of every city where he went. He was not retiring or exclusive; where beauty, pleasure and music met, he mads a feast. He was his own best interpreter of his works. To hear Dunbar read from Dunbar's works, with his deep rich baritone voice, with every action suited to the word, was to see him' at his best and to hold forever afterward a pleasant memory that cannot fade.

A spirit so highly strung and sensitive as his was not without its tragedies. He has come to our study wearing a look of almost hopeless dejection and begged us to come upon our knees alone with him, in the presence of the Alone, to pray for strength and heaven's gracious favor. We have it told elsewhere how he wrought and what, up to now, is the world's estimate of his genius, and we have here, too, an intimate sketch from one who for the first time breaks her silence to speak of him who first won her hand and linked her name forever with his fame.

Phyllis Wheatley and Dunbar, each of the pure African type, were the first to enter the enchanted ground of poesy and song. Up there among "the choir invisible," with Elizabeth Barrett Browning, with Burns and Keats, with Shelley and With Poe, may they not await with confidence the day when the gifted children of their people will hold the wrapped attention of the world, while they flood it with their ravishing strains of music and of song?

A Note About the Authors

Alice Dunbar Nelson (1875–1935) was an African American poet, journalist, and political activist. Born in New Orleans to a formerly enslaved seamstress and a white seaman, Dunbar Nelson was raised in the city's traditional Creole community. In 1892, she graduated from Straight University and began working as a teacher in the New Orleans public school system. In 1895, having published her debut collection of poems and short stories, she moved to New York City, where she cofounded the White Rose Mission in Manhattan. Dunbar Nelson married poet Paul Laurence Dunbar in 1898 after several years of courtship, but their union soon proved abusive. She separated from Dunbar—whose violence and alcoholism had become intolerable—in 1902, after which Nelson taught at Howard High School in Wilmington, Delaware for around a decade. She continued to write and earned a reputation as a passionate activist for equality and the end of racial violence. Her one-act play *My Eyes Have Seen* (1918) was published in *The Crisis*, the journal of the NAACP. Dunbar Nelson settled in Philadelphia in 1932 with her third husband Robert J. Nelson and remained in the city until her death. Her career is exemplified by a mastery of literary forms—in her journalism, stories, plays, and poems, she made a place for herself in the male-dominated world of the Harlem Renaissance while remaining true to her vision of political change and social uplift for all African Americans.

William S. Scarborough (1852–1926) was an African American scholar. Born in Macon, Georgia, he was the son of a railway worker and an enslaved woman. Educated at Atlanta University and Oberlin College, Scarborough became a teacher of classical languages before returning to Oberlin for his master's degree. Upon graduation, he took on the role of professor at Wilberforce University's classics department, specializing in Ancient Greek. Despite his mastery in the field, and despite his prominence as the president of Wilberforce, Scarborough faced discrimination in 1909 when he was not allowed to attend a meeting of the American Philological Association in Baltimore. Regardless, he continued to publish academic research and led Wilberforce University until 1920. A pioneer in his field, Scarborough was only the third African American to Join the APA and the first to be admitted to the prestigious Modern Language Association.

Reverdy C. Ransom (1861–1959) was an African American minister, socialist, and civil rights activist. Born in Ohio, his mother was African American and his father was Native American. Before being ordained as a minister in the African Methodist Episcopal church, Ransom— who had a wife and child as a young man—studied at Wilberforce University and Oberlin College. An advocate of self-improvement and a devoted anti-capitalist, Ransom became a Christian socialist, emphasizing the radical lessons of Jesus in his ministry and activism. He was a cofounder of the Niagara Movement, a gifted public speaker, a historian and editor for the *A. M. E. Church Review*, and a prominent bishop who served as pastor of churches in New York, Ohio, Illinois, and Massachusetts.

A NOTE FROM THE PUBLISHER

Spanning many genres, from non-fiction essays to literature classics to children's books and lyric poetry, Mint Edition books showcase the master works of our time in a modern new package. The text is freshly typeset, is clean and easy to read, and features a new note about the author in each volume. Many books also include exclusive new introductory material. Every book boasts a striking new cover, which makes it as appropriate for collecting as it is for gift giving. Mint Edition books are only printed when a reader orders them, so natural resources are not wasted. We're proud that our books are never manufactured in excess and exist only in the exact quantity they need to be read and enjoyed.

bookfinity™

Discover more of your favorite classics with Bookfinity™.

- Track your reading with custom book lists.
- Get great book recommendations for your personalized Reader Type.
- Add reviews for your favorite books.
- AND MUCH MORE!

Visit **bookfinity.com** and take the fun Reader Type quiz to get started.

Enjoy our classic and modern companion pairings!

Classic & Modern

www.ingramcontent.com/pod-product-compliance
Lightning Source LLC
Chambersburg PA
CBHW020446030426
42337CB00014B/1415